ical book of
moments

vol. II

Jeff Chandler

Copyright © 2016 Jeff Chandler

All rights reserved. No part of this publication may be reproduced, distributed, or transmitted in any form or by any means, including photocopying, recording, or other electronic or mechanical methods, without the prior written permission of the author.

ISBN: 978-1523453054

DEDICATION

For the beautiful, fragile planet we call home – may we find peace and compassion upon you.

CONTENTS

Prologue	1
Sun and Samba	6
Unseen	8
Andalusian Evening	10
Surrender	12
Slowly, But Surely	14
Rainy Tuesday	16
Swings and Roundabouts	18
Morning Chatter	20
Just Visiting	22
Loop	24
On Guard	26
Connected	28
A Perfect Drama	30
Driving Blind	32

Gone Fishing	34
Living the Dream	36
The Pursuit	38
The Freckle	40
Sunshine After the Rain	42
Noodles	44
Brace, Brace	46
Desert Lights	48
Travelling Companion	50
Back to the Future	52
Spring Forward	54
Stroll	56
Step by Step	58
Box Fresh	60
Seasonal Sounds	62
Scars	64
The Flower and the Weed	66

5-a-Day	68
Something Extra	70
B.F.F	72
Ensemble	74
Been There	76
Disappearing Dusk	78
Spectacular Spectacles	80
Changing Flights	82
Alignment	84
First	86
Silent White	88
Click, Flash	90
Homeward Bound	92
About the Author	95

ACKNOWLEDGMENTS

Firstly, without my family of blog followers who sit down every week to read my words, this book wouldn't even exist. Through your stories and kind messages, you have become my inspiration in all manner of ways.
To my wonderful friends and family who give me all the love and support I could ever ask for, thank you from the bottom of my heart.
And to the shining little ones in my life; my nephews, nieces and Godchildren - may your spirits stay forever young and your smiles remain bright.
For the ones I've loved and lost, I will always carry you around, somewhere inside my beating heart.

And once again I am eternally grateful to you, Sean, for giving this book the most beautiful illustrations. You are truly amazing.

PROLOGUE

Last night I had a dream…

I was standing on a tall, white platform suspended high above the ground. A warm Atlantic breeze blew though my hair and whistled over my ears. Patches of green grass and a deep blue ocean spread out as far as the eye could see.

As I walked along the metal gangway, a sudden rush of vertigo hit me as I glanced through the gridded floor. My hand gripped the railing. Continuing on through the dizziness, I followed the bright yellow arrows stencilled at my feet. I walked up towards the steel double doors of the small white room and stepped inside. The area was packed full of electronic equipment. Curly wires, gauges and cubby holes adorned the walls. On the other side of the room was a small padded hole, barely big enough to crawl through.

I climbed in and pulled myself along on my back. It wasn't until I came out the other side that I realised I was on-board a space shuttle.

All around me, illuminated panels of switches and displays flashed randomly. Everything there had its place and reason for being.

Next thing I knew, I was sat in one of the seats as the harness came over my shoulders and was pulled tightly across my waist.

As I surveyed the cockpit, I could hear a bustle of activity behind me from the other crew members. Unable to turn around to see what was going on, I just sat there and gazed forward. Lost in my thoughts, I wondered how I had got there. I was suddenly jolted out of my trance by a deep, metallic thud. The hatch was closed and sealed into place…and then there was nothing. For a moment, all I could hear through my helmet was the low crackle of airwaves and the beating heart inside my chest. It pounded up into my throat. I swallowed.

Then the remainder of a countdown rang through my ears. All my senses were attacked at once as the main engine fired up. We began to shake violently in our seats.

4…3…2…1… Explosively emancipated from the bolts holding us down, we had lift-off. As we cleared the tower, the G-Force pinned me tightly into my seat; I couldn't move. Higher and higher we climbed. I could feel the incredible power of the rockets taking me further than I had ever been before.

My mind raced a thousand miles per hour as it it tried to catch up with the increasing velocity. We thundered through the sky like a comet.

An occasional flash of bright afternoon sunlight glared through the small side window as we twisted towards the blackness of space.

There was nothing except the silent roar of the solid rocket boosters as they burnt the last of their fuel and finally detached. As I turned my head, I could see them outside falling away to make their lonely journey back down to Earth. I wondered how long it would take before they eventually smashed into the cold water below, tangled in their parachutes.

The unbearable pressure of gravity on my body slowly began to subside as we broke away from the dense atmosphere. I watched my arm drift up and float away from my lap.

And on we travelled, out into the unending darkness. The shuttle gently turned. Bright sun burned through the windows and I watched its light glide elegantly across the floor. I looked back. There it was: spinning peacefully in space, with an incredible grace - our beautiful blue planet. My heart skipped a beat and everything suddenly stopped. Hundreds of miles deep into the vacuum, I was speechless. Our shining home - the most incredible thing I have ever seen. I saw continents and oceans and clouds and forests. I watched raging storms and flashes of lightning. I saw the sun rise and sun set. Everything happening all at once, so delicate through the atmospheric glow.

And then it hit me: the stunning realisation that we are all one - one giant family living in amongst the stars. We laugh and cry and breathe the same way. We sleep and dream and hope and pray. And in amongst it all, there are moments - single moments that make up a life. Some happen so quickly; they're barely noticed at all. And then there are others that almost take our breath away; the ones that seem to change our trajectory, forever.

The world is spinning at such a rate, moments can come and go in a flash - they've disappeared before we know it.

With 7.4 billion of us living out here, I began to see the infinite possibilities for change. Every day brings a new opportunity for peace, love and compassion. It's the gift of life.

And as I rested my forehead on the glass, looking out, we floated on through the cosmos; weightless, free, unencumbered - a part of the celestial dance, surrounded by nothing….and everything.

So, here's to you and your little moments. May you always feel the sun on your face and the wind in your hair. May you dance in your living room, sing in the shower and laugh till your cheeks hurt. Be free with the words "I love you", even if they're not returned. Notice the random acts of kindness happening every day. Be kind and gentle with yourself. And smile at strangers – for we are all friends who have not yet met, and everyone is fighting a battle we know nothing about.
But above all, more than anything, I wish you happiness of the heart. You are far more precious than you will ever know!

I love you.

SUN AND SAMBA

I'm up on the 11th floor looking down. The buzz of the city wafts up on currents of warm Brazilian air and carries with it bouncing Samba beats from musicians at a private party down below. Today I spotted my first wild Parakeet. Flapping gracefully past the lush foliage, its beautiful bright green wings seemed to glint in the early evening sun.
And today I had my first Caipirinha - the lime infused cocktail that made my taste buds explode and awakened my senses. I smiled as we stepped out of the bar and back into the sun.
The streets of London seem like a million miles away now. I crossed over the Western Sahara and the Atlantic Ocean just to be here. And now that I've arrived, the world suddenly seems a few degrees brighter than it did just a few short days ago.

The sun, that I adore so much, beats gently down onto my body as it gratefully laps up every last ray. A sudden wave of happiness rushes over me as I realise that I'm right where I'm meant to be.

They say that home is where the heart is, and as I think about all the people in my life that I love so very dearly, I see that no matter where I go, and whatever I do, I will always carry them around with me in my heart - never leaving, nested inside my travelling home.

UNSEEN

The woman struggling with her dog, picking up poo, doesn't see the man in the car reading a map. Lost in the page, he doesn't see the joggers whizz by in their fluorescent Lycra. Eyes forward, they are blind to the teenager on the other side playing keep-up with the ball at the traffic lights.
The wind picks up, swirling a little light dust up into the Brazilian midday air.
And it continues on.
The little girl, holding her mummy's hand across the road, is oblivious to the woman paying for the full tank of gas and a pack of mint chewing gum. She can't see the green parakeet land in a branch overhead, or the black cat running along a crumbling wall.
And none of them see me sitting in a grey car surrounded by traffic; still, invisible, witnessing.
As I look around at the snapshot of the city, I begin to think about the billions of people all living under a single blue sky. Everything we can ever imagine is happening right at this very minute. People are loving

and people are dying; people are laughing and people are trying. Moments of people's lives rush through my mind – separate, yet connected.

A horn blasts up ahead and traffic begins to move once again.

The woman with her dog, the lost man, the footballer, the child, the chewing gum lady, parakeet and cat all disappear from sight, forever. The moment is over.

The city rushes by my window and I'm suddenly pulled into in a song that jumps out from the radio. As I begin to join in, I can't help but wonder if someone is watching the man in the grey car, lost in the music, smiling and singing like no one is watching.

ANDALUSIAN EVENING

There's only a few minutes left of day. The air is changing right in front of my very eyes. Soon, the sun will be gone and I will be indoors, sitting beside a roaring fire.
The mountains begin to turn a deep shade of red.
I tip my head backwards and see white contrails cutting diagonally across a dusky sky. I follow the plane's journey as it makes its way over the mountain to disappear from sight. I wonder about all the people up there; some will be reading, some watching a movie, some dozing lightly.
In the distance, a pack of dogs bark as a chainsaw revs up. There is smoke billowing from a blaze somewhere up in the mountains.
And I breathe in deeply. The delicate scent of pink almond blossom rushes into my nose as I realise that change has come in…. again.
It was so warm today, I felt my body relax and soak up every last ray of Andalusian sun. But now I zip up

my jacket against the chilled evening air.
And as the birds make their final flight of the day back towards their nest, I pick up my phone and empty coffee cup to make my way indoors. Just as I am about to head up along the dusty path, something makes me stop. There, just poking out from behind a eucalyptus tree, sits a gigantic moon. And so I stand there for a while, holding my things, looking up into the evening sky. As a cool breeze blows through the trees, I can't help but feel that everything is exactly as it should be.

SURRENDER

One step at a time, I slowly climb towards the top. Pausing at the first platform, I look out to the narrow white board. The higher I climb, the faster my heart beats until I reach the peak. Shuffling my way to the edge, my stomach lurches into my throat as I look down. Everything moves closer and further away simultaneously in true Hitchcock style. Attacking birds would seem like butterflies right now.
And so I stand there, frozen. Electricity coursing through my veins, I nervously smooth the hair out of my eyes and take a deep breath. I am at least relieved to see that I'm alone up here. I had made it my personal mission, my challenge of spirit to do this dive - turning back was not an option.
And so I close my eyes to the world. The smell of chlorine wafts up from the water below and enters my lungs. I could fight this or I could surrender.
Taking another deep breath, I lean forward as gravity

suddenly grabs my body and pulls me down with his strong hands. I travel through the air with such velocity that everything blurs away.
And I'm powerless.
I slice the water and journey deep into the blue. I keep on going, further than I have ever been before. It is wonderful. Freeing.
As much as we would like, there are some things we just can't control. Whether it be love, life or everything in-between, once we let go and surrender, we open ourselves up to exciting new possibilities. Sometimes, we don't always get what we want, but if we're lucky, we get just what we need.

SLOWLY, BUT SURELY

My friend is old - very old. He makes me chuckle.
As we both enter the manicured garden, he sinks his head into his dark shell to acclimatise. Within a few seconds, my bare feet hit the cool grass and feel instantly refreshed. Gently placing him down, I watch as his little head pops back out of hiding to stretch his neck out once more.
A beautiful day for a stroll.
I am mesmerised by him. The way he looks around and surveys his surroundings brings a smile to my face. He is at peace in his home - his home in which he has lived for decades, is his familiar. His little legs move slowly forward, dragging his bulky shell along one step at a time. He ambles over to investigate the giant, now sitting on the grass with him. Touching my leg with his head, he looks up. I know what he loves. I come bearing gifts. One by one, he munches on delicious strawberry tops and juicy dandelion heads. He is slow and elegant and lovely.
As he continues to feast, I watch and wonder about how fast everything seems to be spinning in the

world. We text as we walk, work as we fly, and eat on the run. At times, it's easy to feel lost and overwhelmed by our gigantic juggling act. We all have hopes and dreams and places to be. But as much as we push forward and strive to achieve, sometimes we just need to stop for a moment and take stock. A little time to simply breathe and be. Comfortable in our own shell.

And once we slow down just enough to look around, we might just realise we are closer to our dreams than we thought.

RAINY TUESDAY

Tuesday evening rain splashes down onto cold pavement. It has been like this all day and looks set to carry on into the night.
As the door to my office clicks shut behind me, I breathe deeply and watch my umbrella pop open.
And so begins the commute home towards drawn blinds, soft lighting and a comfy sofa.
I love these moments! With music pulsing through headphones down into my ears, I join the strangers on the street, and walk. I can't remember the last time I didn't feel at home here. Nights of being alone and scared in a big city seem like a lifetime ago now.
As I approach the corner to cross, I notice a massive muddy puddle spilling out from the curb into the road. I know this corner and I see what's coming...
As I take a step back away from the edge, people around me suddenly understand my movement and follow me in quick succession. We share a knowing smile with each other just as the bus trundles past and splashes the puddle up and out.

These funny moments of random connection remind me that we are all related.

And so I continue on towards the tube. I know that it will be packed down there this evening. A wave of peace washes over me in anticipation of the warm cocoon that awaits. I can get lost in the crowd once again and feel the mass of beating hearts.

We see so many people every day on our journey, some familiar, some not. Sometimes paths cross to turn into something more meaningful, and sometimes one glance is all we ever have.

And as I begin my descent into the ticket hall, I can't help but wonder where all these strangers are off to tonight. Strangers with their dripping umbrellas and soggy newspapers.

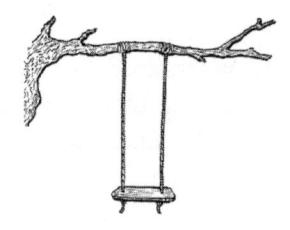

SWINGS AND ROUNDABOUTS

1, 2, 3, 4, 5, 6, 7, 8, 9, 10 – Coming ready or not...

All my friends had disappeared into the fast approaching sunset, never to be seen again (unless I looked in the bush and up the tree but why spoil their fun so soon). I remember how long those summer evenings were, stretching into forever.
As adults, we sometimes forget what it was like to be a child and instead, wear our bodies with a heaviness that does nothing to free our spirit. Feeling bogged down by day jobs and expectations, the brightness and lightness of the real us slowly gets hidden under a layer of dusty conformity.
There is something in the way that children can look at this beautiful world we live in and know, without a single doubt, that every moment holds infinite possibilities. I think that the little ones might just be onto something. Imagine waking up tomorrow and

seeing everything currently in our lives as an amazing opportunity to fly. How freeing that would be!
So when the next challenge comes merrily along, stop for a second and try to see it through different eyes. Let's listen to our inner child for once. They may be young but they are very wise.

Last one to the tree has to buy the sweets…

MORNING CHATTER

Sunday morning and a chorus of Wood Pigeons call in the distance. It is the first thing I hear as I wake. Still dozy from sleep, I listen as one repeats the same three notes over and over again. Then another joins in, this time with five. It is all I hear until they suddenly stop. Stillness.
In the silence I yawn. My tummy rumbles. And the pigeons return. Then a Crow. Then a Sparrow. Then something else I can't identify: a strange, deep squawk. It was definitely a bird of sorts, but not one that I have heard before. Or maybe it was a child.
As I listen to the orchestra of sounds, my mind suddenly skips back to another time: London Zoo, a light drizzle falling onto my face as I stood listening to the Peacocks. Trying hard to mimic their call, I began repeating back exactly what I heard, subtly adjusting the quality of my sound each time until eventually we merged and became one. I smile at the memory of seeing the rest of my drama school friends all doing the same thing. The next day we would find ourselves back together in class, all laughing at the

strange looks we received from the rest of the visitors around us, before making the room come alive once again with lions, and tigers, and Peacocks, oh my!
I chuckle at the seeming randomness of life.
And as the birds continue to chatter outside my window, in between the squawking and singing, I begin to drift off once again into a deep morning sleep.

JUST VISITING

I used to think I had just one pace in this city when I first arrived. Two decades later, I've discovered another. There are times in our life when all we can do is let go and allow the current to take us where it will. With nowhere else to get to for at least another hour, I slow my stride and begin to melt in amongst the strangers. Between shoulder bags and cameras and shorts and smiles, I snatch glimpses of a city I love - foreign to my crowd, familiar to me. Big Ben glints in the early evening sunset behind red buses, black cabs, and bicycles.

I stop occasionally as tourists in front of me pose wearily against a sunset skyline; a long day of walking and exploring finally taking its toll. I watch as they soak everything in. It will soon be time for them to head back to their hotel to shower and change before heading out again for dinner.

Once across the river, I find myself retreating to the park opposite Westminster. This is my favourite part of killing time - I love people watching. The blonde-haired girl cartwheels freely across the grass and heads towards the Japanese couple freezing for a picture with their fingers held playfully in a peace sign - I love this pose. Maybe deep down, that's all the majority of us want for the planet anyway. There are kids playing around the bronze statue now and I chuckle to myself as they hold onto the giant finger to dance with it. Their laughter rings out across the grass, becoming part of the city soundtrack.

A Union Jack blows gently in the breeze high upon a rooftop.

Suddenly a bee buzzes sleepily past and I follow its journey around behind me. I realise that I've been sitting right in front of a wall of lavender this whole time. And so I reach behind to squeeze a piece in between my fingers. The scent fills my nostrils and floods me with happiness.

And everything's perfect.

LOOP

Higher and higher we climb. The chain rattling and clunking beneath the carriage lets me know that we're not quite at the top yet. Wind begins to swirl around and dance through my hair. It feels so nice in spite of the adrenaline that is coursing through my veins. For a brief moment I wonder if we will ever stop climbing. My heart continues to beat out of my chest as the world suddenly turns silent. From up here I can see for miles. Over the treetops and rides below, people look like ants on the ground: funny, strange, busy. A beautiful deep blue sky frames everything. And then, ever so slowly,
we
begin
to
fall.
My grip on the side bars tighten and my knuckles change colour. Accelerating at warp speed, the world suddenly becomes a blur as I'm lost in the fall. Head pushed back into my seat, we spiral and turn and rattle and shake. Faster and faster we go.

It is just before we hit the loop that I notice some people in front of me with their arms raised high above their heads. A scream of excitement rings out up ahead and with a deep breath, for the first time, I let go. Hands free, I float them high above my head as wind rushes through my fingertips.

Then I realise in that moment that I am laughing loudly. And on we travel, tipping and turning around every bend. I feel so light, free.

After one last exhilarating dip, we begin to decelerate and pull into the platform once again.

With the safety bar released and lifted up off my torso, I step out of the carriage and make my way down the wooden steps. My mind continues to race at a hundred miles an hour.

As I look over my shoulder at the place we've just been, high above the earth, I can't help but think about the times I've tried to hold on so tightly to things before. The fear of losing people I love is palpable.

But that's the thing about life. We grow, we change, we laugh, we cry. Things don't always go smoothly, and we can't control everything. But as long as we keep our hands and hearts open, safety bar or not, we are always going to be ok. Everything that is truly meant to be, happens in its own time and place. And whether we hold on tightly to the bar or wave our arms up in the air, there will always be bright new beginnings just around the next bend.

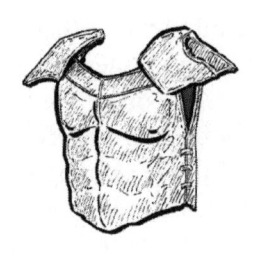

ON GUARD

It would definitely shatter a bone, or two. The heavy iron end would smash through anything that got in its way. The protruding spikes are blunt and weighty. A shiver runs down my spine as I picture how many people have been on the receiving end of its deathly blow.
Next to it sits the beautifully crafted rifles. Delicately decorated in Mother of Pearl, it is hard to imagine that something so aesthetically pleasing was made to kill.
There are silver daggers, steel swords, and pocketknives, all designed to swipe and chop and slice and stab.
Gazing through the glass case that protects the protective armour, I admire the craftsmanship of the smooth metallic suit. Every piece, hammered and shaped perfectly to fit the contours of a body.
As I continue walking around the armoury room of the Wallis Collection, I am suddenly struck by a thought: for all the ways we protect ourselves in war -

the shields, the armour, the heavy weaponry - what about the everyday? How do we protect ourselves against the many other dangers that lie in wait? There are times in life when I could have done with an emotional coat of armour myself. I would have made use of its thick steel skin as a heavy defence – that way my feelings would never have been hurt, my heart never broken, or my confidence battered.
Life can be messy and disorientating sometimes. But as long as we love ourselves with all our imperfections, and protect our heart by keeping it open, that might just be all the armour we will ever need.

CONNECTED

I love this time of day. The bustling city is changing gears to find another pace. Final splashes of golden sun illuminates the grass below and casts shadows across the lawn as I sit looking out. Within a few short minutes, day will become night once more. I watch the last rays of evening light gently cover the city in its golden blanket, and even though there is still a pale blue sky, the street lamps have already come on to see us through the small hours.
Today I saw a picture of the earth taken from beneath Saturn's rings. And today I saw a picture of a train wreck - I will go to sleep this night, a different person. As I look down towards my hands, I suddenly notice the orange stains from the dead lilies that I placed into the bin earlier. An image of the child presenting the bouquet to me last week flashes through my mind, making me smile; gestures of kindness and gratitude that will never be forgotten.
I read somewhere earlier that London was hotter than Bali! These warm summer days quickly give way to

cool nights, and as a chill blows across my skin, I realise that the shadows are no more; we have spun away from the sun.

I contemplate going inside for a hot Green Tea when a thought occurs to me: In this moment, everything is happening. With 7.4 billion of us all sharing this planet, we are connected in ways we don't even know - variations of a theme with beating hearts and hopes and fears. We are family.

And as I make my way inside to put the kettle on, I know I'm not the only one.

A PERFECT DRAMA

Beautiful men and glamorous women drink out of champagne flutes and talk in a language I don't understand. I watch as words float poetically out of their perfect mouths and I'm caught up in the elegance.
Someone says something...and suddenly everything stops. The room falls silent as mouths fall open. Something is seriously wrong! What is going on? My brain can't make sense of the situation. After a minute or so of stunned silence, the screaming begins. Guests lash out at one other and start to claw viciously at expensive clothes and blow-dried hair. I need to know what's going on.
After some much needed translation from a friend, it turns out that the gathering was a pre-wedding dinner for the daughter who was unknowingly about to marry her father. Then she finds out that he was not actually her real father anyway.
Alongside this, it was revealed that the man with perfect eyebrows had watched his sister deliver a baby in a bar toilet and had taken the baby off her to give

to someone else to adopt. Well, now it turns out that he actually put the baby in a skip and left it there...well, that would account for the hysterics.
My jaw is on the floor!
The mother of the man with the perfect eyebrows disowns her son and he is pushed forcefully down the stairs into the broken glass...
And then the credits roll against a backdrop of dramatic music.
I might just have witnessed the best telenovela in history, ever!
Laughing loudly with the theme tune, I realise something: no matter how difficult and challenging life can be sometimes, compared to what I've just witnessed, I'm living a doce vida.
And it's blissfully simple!

DRIVING BLIND

And suddenly my ears pop - the sweet release of pressure.
Two and a half hours after leaving the city, we begin to snake our way up through the mountain. I love to watch the world whizz by, lost in my thoughts.
People and places wash in and out of my mind like a summer tide.
The weather is changing. Gone are the blue skies of earlier to be replaced by something else.
Carefully navigating a tight bend in the road, everything is suddenly smothered by a thickening white fog as horizon vanishes right in front of our very eyes. The car slows to a crawl as an eerie silence descends. I suddenly remember the foggy morning in East London that concealed Canary Wharf from view; a lost moment in time that now lives safely in my heart, forever.
Higher and higher we drive, embraced tightly by the fog.

And my mind is racing. I can't help but wonder if, with all the challenges and choices in life, we don't all get lost in the fog sometimes. There are days when the sky is cloudless, blue - we know exactly where we are going. And then there are times when we just can't see the wood for the trees.

But sometimes a fog is there to remind us that as long as we stay true to ourselves and trust our intuition, we will eventually find our way out through.

And just when I think that we are never going to get out of this, we turn a corner and discover a bright burning sun once more.

GONE FISHING

I didn't know if it was the beer, the blazing sun, or a combination of the two, but I suddenly felt sleepy out on the river bank. It was nice to be away from the city for a few days, and for the first time in ages, I felt my mind soften around the edges.
As I finished the last of my drink, my friend turned to ask if I fancied doing a spot of fishing. A smile crept across my face as I found myself out on the deck of their narrow boat. After a quick lesson in the basics, my friend hopped back onto solid ground...and there I stood, alone in my thoughts, looking out across the river. The peacefulness of that moment was beautiful!
It didn't last long!
I watched the lure fly gracefully out across the water to land with a gentle splash once again...then I felt my line pull, hard. The rod began to bend, and for a moment, I wondered if I had managed to get it caught again on some weeds at the bottom. Within a few seconds, to my absolute horror, I pulled the line

out of the water and found myself staring at a thrashing 25lb Pike!

With that, I screamed, my friends came running, and passers-by stopped to see what was causing such a commotion. And so the battle to release the giant began.

The mere sight of its razor-sharp teeth coming towards me was enough to have me climbing up the railing away from it.

After what seemed like an age of twisting and struggling, I watched my friend bend down to place him back into the water from whence he came. He was finally home. Safe. Free.

Then as I looked down through the ripples, laughing with relief, I realised something: In life, there will always be challenges. Things happen unexpectedly to take us on a different journey. Sometimes we find ourselves in an unimagined future.

And that night, as I looked out of the car window into the starry sky, I couldn't help but smile. This would forever be the day that I wrestled with a river monster, and won!

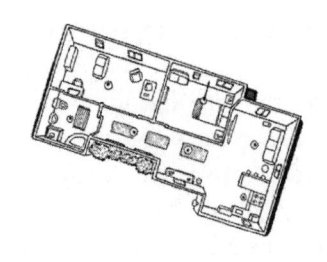

LIVING THE DREAM

The first wall goes up easily. A wall turns into a room. A room turns into a house. Wallpaper up and a hardwood floor down, the stylish furniture goes in. A bed, a sofa, a TV, a coffee machine. Sun shining, pink blossom trees get planted around the poolside without a single bead of sweat ever falling from my brow.
Then I move in.
I walk over to the wardrobe which sits next to the beautiful flowers and slip into smart-casual. Nice. Then my dog arrives. She loves her new home. After a quick look around she immediately begins to dig a hole in the freshly-mowed lawn. I am not bothered. I am too busy chatting to my new acquaintance. We become friends. Then with a single kiss, we become something else. He is perfect.
Without realising, I find myself lost in a moment of creating the perfect life. Only it's not a real life. Hitting the save button, I close the game down and take a sip of my coffee. And as I sit there enjoying a few minutes of peace, I can't help but think about all the things in life that I have yet to achieve - hopes and

dreams that live deep in my heart. I wonder what they will look like. Will they be how I imagined? Or something else entirely? And in amongst all the things I want, lies everything that I really need; the things that help me to grow, to laugh, to learn, to change. I suddenly get the feeling that I haven't even scratched the surface. Sometimes we think we know exactly what we need in life, the things that will bring us happiness. And sometimes we are right on the money. But occasionally we need to let go of everything we think we know in order to open ourselves up to new opportunities.

And maybe, just maybe, everything we need has been right under our nose the whole time.

THE PURSUIT

And the game had begun. In hot pursuit of the suspect, I ran as fast as I could past my friend's front door, with peeling red paint, past the corner shop selling all my favourite Cola Cubes, over the grass hill peppered with daisies upon which we occasionally danced, and out onto the small side street sloping all the way down towards the nursery. Approaching the only parked car on the quiet street, my walkie-talkie crackled with white noise as something caught my eye. It glinted in the afternoon sun. I stopped suddenly to investigate, blocking out the voice now coming out over the airwaves. And there at my feet lay £10,000,000 worth of sparkling princess cut diamonds!
Scooping them up carefully into my hands, I poured them into a pocket and got straight onto the walkie-talkie to excitedly announce that I had discovered the abandoned treasure from the heist. Ignoring the brick inside the car that had shattered the window into a million pieces the night before by a vandal, it was

definitely the find of the century in this make-believe moment.

Years later, I smile back at those long summer days of playing cops and robbers until the sun went down, and of the time that broken glass was magically transformed into a thousand beautiful diamonds. Sometimes in life we get so lost in the pursuit of happiness, we can miss the beautiful moments that are already all around, glinting in the sun, just waiting to be discovered.

FRECKLE

There is a freckle. It lives on the inside of my middle finger, right hand. It has been there for as long as I can remember and I don't even know the first time I became aware of it.
Despite being there for all to see, I'm pretty sure there's no one on this planet who knew about its existence. Even those who have been intimately close with me probably won't have noticed it at all.
But it's there.
It has been with me every step of the way. It was there the morning I jumped off the train and landed in London. There the first time I took off into the sky. There the day I fell in love and there the night my heart was broken. It has seen me across vast oceans and sprawling continents, through burning sun and pouring rain. It has listened to me laugh and cry and sing and scream. Felt grains of warm sand trickle over it and the petals of a red rose rest on it.
With billions of us on this beautiful blue planet, it is easy to feel like just another face in the crowd. We

meet so many people at different stages of our life - some become friends, some, lovers, and some just pass on quickly through.

But wherever we go and whoever we meet on our journey, as long as we remember that there is no one else on this planet exactly like us, and we love every freckle on our body, we will always shine.

SUNSHINE AFTER THE RAIN

Warm Sunday morning sun begins to dry off the remaining drops of water that glisten on the green leaves below. It rained again in the night. The hypnotic beating on my bedroom window usually sends me into a deep sleep within minutes.
Fresh coffee in hand, I sit on my balcony and look out. It has been a tough week and, for the first time in ages, I completely fill my lungs with air and notice how instantly my muscles thank me for it.
Regardless of all the challenges we face and all the mountains we have to climb, life still goes on. The Earth hasn't stopped spinning. Neither has the canal, meandering gently past. And birds continue to sing joyfully overhead with a song I don't quite understand, but love none the less.
I notice a tiny spider descending slowly down a single piece of silvery thread towards her newly built web. She must have set to work early this morning as soon as the rain had stopped falling.

And there is blue sky above once again. There has been so much rain lately, it seemed like the sky would be forever grey.

It is easy to get lost in our daily struggles and bogged down in our thoughts…but nothing happens for nothing. I can't help but wonder if the key to happiness and everything else we seek, has been hiding behind the clouds the whole time.

NOODLES

The first time I met her she licked my face and ran behind a chair.
Every now and then she would come over to me with those curious brown eyes to investigate. Her teeth, like tiny needles, would close playfully down on my hand making me chuckle. And then after a long day of exploring, she would climb up onto my lap and fall asleep. Her heartbeat slowed and I would watch her little body expand and contract with every breath. She seemed so vulnerable.
After a few weeks she grew stronger and more confident. It was time for her first walk outside. I cradled her up in my arms and closed the door behind me. We walked down the hill towards the common. I smiled as she took in every last detail of the outside world.
I was madly in love.
Within a couple of days, she had struck up a friendship with one of the older regulars. I smiled at the way she would sniff his face and run away slowly,

knowing that she could easily outrun her new friend if she wanted to. Watching this little one with stiffened joints running happily after the cheeky puppy was heart-warming. They had their understanding.

Then one day, after a rough-and-tumble session with another puppy, Noodles hurt her paw. She let out a yelp and limped her way over towards me. I scooped her up in my arms and hugged her tightly. Suddenly she seemed so delicate, fragile.

As I carried her home, I began to think about our journey through life and our connections to each other.

That day, I was reminded how important it is to show tenderness, compassion and love towards others. For at some point in our life, we too will need others to do the same for us.

BRACE, BRACE

"Ladies and gentlemen, your attention - for your safety be aware of the following: A safety card is in your seat pocket showing the exit routes, oxygen masks, life jackets, and brace position that you must adopt if you hear 'brace, brace'. There are two emergency exits at the rear, four in the middle and two at the front of the cabin".

As we pull away from the terminal and crawl towards the end of the runway, I look out of the window. The early morning sky is already a beautiful shade of blue. Soon I will be lifted from the earth, high above the clouds once more. My mind begins to wander up and out of the cabin to a place filled with an Orange Blossom breeze and a burning sun.

"Floor lighting will guide you to an exit. Be aware of your nearest exit. In an emergency leave all cabin baggage on-board".

With engines full throttle and seconds before the

brakes are released, a thought occurs to me: in the event of an inflight crisis, we will be fully prepared with everything we need to know to help us get through it.

But what if the air supply doesn't fail, or we don't land on water. What if the emergency is invisible to everyone else but ourselves? How do we brace for the agony of a heartbreak, the loss of a loved one, a job, a dream, or the countless other challenges that life throws at us on a daily basis? Where is the life jacket, oxygen mask and low level lighting then?

Sometimes in life things pop up to throw us off track. We think we will never again be able to open our hearts, or dare to dream, or give in to hope. But with every knock-back comes a new beginning; an opportunity to learn a lesson and shine brighter than ever before.

777

DESERT LIGHTS

As the lift doors slide open, a wave of bright light and electronic noise smashes into me. I step out into the hotel casino and my senses are suddenly stimulated. Snaking my way through the endless rows of hypnotic slot machines, I slow for a moment to watch the woman with her back to me. Mesmerised by flashing lights and spinning wheels, she reaches into her large plastic cup without looking and pulls out a handful of quarters. One by one she delicately feeds them into the slot and continues to push random buttons. She must be doing something right, for no sooner as she does this, a handful more are spewed out the bottom. She barely cracks a smile and I can't help but wonder how long she has been sitting there - it is still only 8.30am.
I chuckle for her.
As I continue onwards past green poker tables and spinning roulette wheels, I notice that there is something very warm and cosy about being in this surreal bubble. The lack of any natural light just adds to my sense of disorientation.

Walking through the lobby and out of a revolving door, the burning sun instantly warms my face and it takes a few seconds for my eyes to adjust to the new light.

I am suddenly struck by the peculiarity of standing in the middle of a desert, surrounded by all of this. I love the randomness of it all. And right on cue as I turn the corner, two Lycra-clad superheroes walk casually past, sipping their Starbucks as they make their way to work.

In a few short days I will be back home again. But right now, I'm here in the sparkling oasis.

And it's glorious.

TRAVELLING COMPANION

The first time I ever laid eyes on you, you were looking out through a window on Charing Cross Road. I knew instantly that you were the one. I stepped in from the cold…and the rest is history. Our history - it was all meant to be. I will never forget the moments that we've spent together. My faithful one. You were there when I first stepped foot onto Italian soil, and there as I walked into a wall of Brazilian heat. We've seen sleepy romantic lakes and exciting new cities. I've lost count of the number of hotel rooms we've slept in over the years. The familiar click of a heavy door shutting behind us will stay with me forever.

We've been on quite a journey, you and I.

Do you remember the times we ran through airport with seconds to spare? Or those where we soared peacefully above oceans below?

We've struggled over cobbles and glided over concrete; travelled on tracks and roads and currents of air. You've been lifted and pulled and dragged and thrown. And still you stayed right by my side. There as I cried in the rain. And kissed in the dark. And

laughed on a train. And fell. And got back up.
So seeing your handle finally broken and sitting next to the bin makes me a little sad - sad that you will never again be hauled off a carousel in a brand new country. And sad that you won't get to see my face as I laugh once again at the little moments that life can bring.
But with every ending comes a new beginning.
And I look forward to the day when you return, in a different form, to once again run with me through an airport with seconds to spare.

BACK TO THE FUTURE

This afternoon I time travelled.
It came like a bolt out of the blue. Trees and pavement instantly melted away and before I knew it I had been grabbed and thrown backwards into 1989. Verse to bridge to chorus - each chord holding me tighter and pulling me deeper into the reverie. I watched myself chilling on my single bed, looking up at my prized Kylie poster. Feeling every piece of emotion rush back through my veins, I had no choice but to stay in the moment, reliving every second of a first love and a giant dream. Three and a half minutes later, I was back to 2016 with a jolt.
This shuffle button was causing me to leap backwards and forwards erratically without any concern for chronology. I had only just got my bearings when it happened again. 2009 - I observed myself looking out of the tour bus window towards rolling Italian countryside. Engulfed by my history, I passively witnessed it all over again: the warm evening sunset

reflecting off the glass on which I rested my head - it all felt so real. I was back there.

Once again, the song faded out as I was picked up and flicked back to the future. And this continued on for the duration of my journey. Some songs made my stomach ache, some brought a big smile to my face. Music is the soundtrack to our lives, and as we move forward, certain songs will act as a personalised time machine. If we are lucky enough, these tunes will connect us to a moment in our story and be a reminder of how far we've come on our journey and how far we have yet to go.

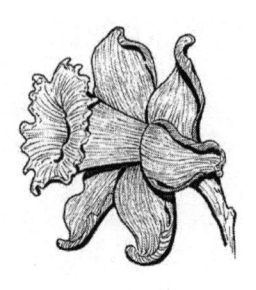

SPRING FORWARD

The air has changed again; days getting longer and evenings, warmer. As I wander along the glistening canal, a swan glides gracefully across the surface and catches my eye. Watching her move through the water, I am lost in time and everything stops still. A memory of me as a boy watching planes thunder down the runway and lift off into the air comes back to me out of absolutely nowhere. I stay there until the sound of a train rattling somewhere in the distance pulls me abruptly back. I continue on. The wind picks up and blows through the weeping willow, making the branches sway majestically. A man jogs past me and for a brief moment I can hear his lungs fill with air and quickly empty. I smile as I suddenly become aware of my own breathing and it occurs to me that we are all built the same; we are one. I can't remember the last time I jogged.

The early evening sun continues to beat down on me and fills me with its final rays of warmth. Soon, the sky will get darker and the air, cooler. In a few short hours I will be turning my clocks forward again before drifting off to sleep. But right now, I'm here, walking along the canal with my bright yellow daffodils.

STROLL

For the first time in ages I am not in a rush. Not late, not hurried, at peace. Dusk is quickly setting in as I stroll along Southbank and up towards the National Theatre.
The remaining rays of evening sun reflect off the rippling water to give everything one last burst of light, before vanishing for another day. Within a few minutes it will be night-time and the illuminated iron lamps will guide the way.
I love it here.
Boats hypnotically snake their way along the current-filled river and I watch as the undulations are momentarily displaced before calming again, leaving no trace whatsoever that the vessels were ever there. And I continue onwards under the protecting canopy of trees, breathing deeply once again as a light evening drizzle blows in and gently places a cool mist onto my face. The city has been harsh lately and I welcome its gentle embrace once again. I have wanted this, needed this.

Sometimes in life, things get difficult. Swallowed up by identical days and freezing nights, it's easy to get lost in the maze. But somewhere, buried deep in the solitude of restlessness, lies something beautiful, calming. We all need these moments of quiet to reset. And as the colourful banners of the theatre come into view, I'm suddenly struck by how important it is to have people in our life who will love us unconditionally and always be there for us when things get tough.

STEP BY STEP

Trainers laced, muscles stretched, I step out into the morning and hit the play button. The beat kicks in and I am off. Snaking my way down towards the canal, a light morning drizzle covers my face. Every stride forward lifts me further out of my sleepiness. I eventually settle into a comfortable pace as the path in front rolls towards my moving feet. I have really been enjoying these early morning runs of late, and despite this only being the third time in my new resolution, I am finding every step just that little bit easier, that little bit faster. A wave of contentment splashes over me as I breathe deeply. Endorphins rush in with a pumping new tune and I decide to speed up my run for a quick burst.

I want to go faster and further.

And just as the song hits the chorus, I accelerate. For a split second it feels as if I am lifting off the ground...and that's when it happens: the sudden searing pain in my left calf.

In less than three seconds, I find myself leaning against a tree with frustration and disappointment crashing heavily into me. How could this have happened? It was game over!

Taking a deep breath, I begin the long journey home, drizzle continuing to fall over my limping body.

And then I realise something...

Sometimes in life, change can take a while. It doesn't always play out like a cleverly cut montage in a movie, and as frustrating as it is, we can't rush the process. The journey is beautiful. With just one perfectly small step, we can take that giant leap right into our very own future.

BOXFRESH

It was a beautiful spring afternoon when I first spotted them. I wasn't even searching - they just appeared out of nowhere.
Completely smitten, I walked through the doorway and stepped onto the escalator. I watched shoppers glide down in the opposite direction, occasionally making eye contact with me.
I made my way over to the wall and plucked them from the shelf. Sitting down, I took off my well-worn shoes and laced up the new ones.
The second I saw their reflection in the mirror, I knew they were meant for me.
I was crazy in love.
And so, later that evening as a burning sunset surrounded us, we stepped out together for the first time.
We danced, carefree, into the early hours of the morning. We went out for brunch the next day, for a walk in the afternoon, and the cinema that evening. It was perfect.

Until they began to hurt. A lot.
Firm leather had started to rub unforgivingly on my ankle and Achilles heel. Every step was agony. The further I walked, the more uncomfortable they became. The sides continued to dig in cruelly, forgetting all the good times we were having together. The honeymoon was over.
I stoically wore them every day that week. Some days were worse than others.
Meanwhile, all around me, flowers were bursting out of the ground and nests were being built high up in the trees.
And then, one day, I noticed that the pain had completely vanished. There was no longer any rubbing or discomfort. All that remained was the gentle click-clack of soles meeting the pavement – just my handsome new shoes and I under a perfect blue sky.
And in amongst the swirling cherry blossom, I suddenly felt very lucky: Lucky to be healthy, alive, and surrounded by love.

SEASONAL SOUNDS

The chandeliers dim and a hush falls over the audience. A scent of dark, solid wood hangs heavy in the air and I watch as candles flicker and dance all around. The orchestra begins to tune their instruments, creating a jumble of chaotic sound. Bows stroke strings and air blows through reed. After a few seconds, silence once again falls through the church.
And so it begins.
A melody written over 400 years ago comes back to life in an instant. As I close my eyes, I wonder how many people have heard this piece over the centuries. Violins, cellos and oboes awaken to create the most beautiful sound that wafts up towards me and falls straight into my heart.
A jarring police siren whizzes past, breaking my peace. I am temporarily reminded that I am surrounded by a bustling city. And as I fall back into the music, I notice that the burning orange sun has

now been replaced by a dusk. I begin to feel even more cosy.
I am suddenly struck that autumn is back. The cool nights will be drawing in and leaves will fall. A pang of sadness washes over me as I realise that I never got a chance to say goodbye to the lovely season.
Something magical happened this summer and I can't shake the feeling that maybe, just maybe, I have been changed forever.

SCARS

As I started running, I knew I could do it. With each stride getting longer and longer, I picked up momentum until I passed the point of no return. The fence wasn't even that high and the section I'd chosen to hurdle over was lower than the rest. Some of the neglected wires seemed to blow in the wind. As my foot touched down for the final time before the leap, something didn't feel quite right. I guess the relentless downpour that morning had changed the ground upon which I ran. With a slip of the foot, my body left the ground and began to sail over the wire fence. Maybe I would clear it after all...
18 stitches and 27yrs. later, I still have my memento of that journey on my right leg.
There is also a place on my left bicep that my little niece has affectionately named 'the soft bit'. She loves to touch it because it feels like a butterfly's wing. Even though I was too young to remember the accident, I still get used as a cautionary tale for the kids to stay away from boiling water.

Throughout our lives, things happen to leave us with

scars. Some are very easy to spot, and others, live on the inside. Whether they come from a leap of faith or a broken heart, these experiences change us forever. But that's ok. Our scars are just a reminder of how strong we really are.

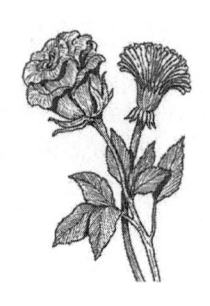

THE FLOWER AND THE WEED

This morning, for the first time in a long time, blazing sun meets me as I step out of the house. A slight breeze on my arms and a warmth on my skin tells me that it's going to be a lovely day. It seemed like the hovering grey clouds above would be a permanent fixture...but they are gone, for now.
And as I walk past the grassy patch to my left, I see the beautiful little things that I used to love. Suddenly thrown back through time, I land in a field of daisies. There was something about the way they looked that always made me smile; like mini flowers growing wild, free.
Endless summers of playing out until the sun went down, of daisy chains, kiss chase, and he-loves-me-he-loves-me-not float through my mind. I suddenly can't remember the last time I sat and played with the daisies...5, 10, 30 years ago?
There was something I heard a long time ago: *'Weeds are just flowers in the wrong place.'*

And as I look up into bright blue sky, I can't help but wonder if the same can't be said of us too. Sometimes in life we find ourselves in the company of people who can leave us feeling less-than. We can doubt our own uniqueness and believe that we're a weed. But that's the wonderful thing about us: we are all special in our own way! And just like the daisies standing wild in the grass, we need to surround ourselves with people who can appreciate our beauty and see us for who we truly are.

5-A-DAY

Feeling the first few drops of cool Autumn rain splash against my skin, I step casually into the quiet cocoon of the supermarket and snatch a basket from the pile as I walk past. Hit by an air-conditioned breeze, I instantly feel refreshed and ready to tackle the maze. And so I move forward into the aisle, suddenly engulfed by towering shelves and eye-catching labels. Plucking items from their metal branches, I place them one by one into my basket and continue onwards. Finally reaching the colourful fruit and vegetables, I stop to run through the list in my head and make my way over to the bright red peppers. My favourite song of the moment begins to play joyfully through blue headphones into my ears and I begin to think about what it means to get our 5-a-day. I have a new routine. My gratitude 5-a-day. Every night as I gently drift off to sleep, I run through the day and pluck out 5 things that I am grateful for: lessons learnt, conversations with friends, being lucky enough to see the sunset.... It's amazing how, once we take a moment to really look at our life, we see how much we really have. Even on our darkest days, there is always something lying just under the surface to be thankful for.

And as I make my way through the checkout and back out towards the exit, I see that the rain is coming down heavily now...and I smile. Soon I will be home, safe and sound, grateful for the food in my bags and the music in my ears.

SOMETHING EXTRA

It happened in the early hours of this morning. I was fast asleep. Eyes closed, breathing deeply, I dreamt about people and places long gone. The streets outside were quiet and deserted as city foxes came out to play in the light of the tall yellow lamps dotted all around. The almost full moon shone brightly, bathing everything in a silvery glow. I wasn't even aware of when the moment arrived. It crept in unannounced, without fanfare and waited patiently for the dawn. My eyes slowly opened to the new day, earplugs pulled out as I came to. And then I noticed its presence. The gift had arrived...

And so I began to think about how I could spend this extra hour. Sixty minutes in our time doesn't seem that much but the possibilities held within it are incredible. We can do something wonderful to set in motion a chain of events that will change the course of our life, forever. We can tell someone that we love them, do something great for someone else or just lie back and enjoy the peace of living in the moment. It is ours to do with whatever we choose. Life is so precious, every moment counts and this bonus of an extra hour comes just at the right time. A time, in which life seems so cramped with stuff, we wish we had more hours in the day...and now, for a short while, we do.

B.F.F

"Friendship with oneself is all-important because without it one cannot be friends with anyone else in the world."
- Eleanor Roosevelt

My best friend and I have always had a tempestuous relationship.
I've known him for years and we have gone through so much together. We've flown across oceans and walked on desert, drank Spritz in Italian piazzas and ate sandwiches in the Grand Canyon. I remember us crying in the dark once at a sad movie and laughing loudly afterwards until it hurt. We have had so much fun.
Some days I really feel his support and his kind words encourage me. Occasionally, when frightened, he will judge me and effortlessly put me down, knowing exactly which buttons to push. Sometimes he tells me that I am not good enough and that I am going to fail,

always directly to my face.

In spite of all this though, I know that he will always be right by my side, forever, and I need to constantly work on the relationship I have with him. He is after all, part of me - my history and my future wrapped into one.

We all have a best friend inside us and it's this relationship which is the most important. We can nurture this friendship in a supportive and loving way so that no matter what, there will always be that confidant with whom we can trust, who will always have our back and tell us that we are good enough and that we can do it!

Be your own BFF.

ENSEMBLE

A light early morning drizzle comes to rest gently on my face. I close the front door and breathe deeply. Pressing play, my short journey begins. I take the shortcut though the passageway towards the common. 'No Doubt' comes playing out of my headphones. It seems that, of late, I've been listening to this album on a loop. In years to come, I wonder if the memories of now will come flooding back the second I hear these songs again.
An old lady comes shuffling along in the opposite direction. With a half-full shopping bag, she looks up at me. We catch each other's eye and for a few seconds we are connected. Her face is gentle and kind. And in our fleeting moment together, we smile. Everything seems to suddenly stop. Then, as she slips out of view, I wonder what she has experienced in life: her hopes, her dreams, her lessons.
I am lost in my thoughts as I continue onwards.
I see the man at the bus stop holding his son's hand - I think of my dad. I see the lady pushing a new-born baby – I think of my friend. I see the guy who looks

like someone I once loved – I wonder where he is now.
Flashes of moments come and go in the drizzle - a Saturday morning stroll through my past.
And as I arrive at the small supermarket, I wonder where my new friend is - the man who sells the Big Issue, with a face that could light up a room, is not there. Maybe I will see him next week.
I suddenly think about all the people in my life - the people who have been there right from the beginning, and the ones who will be there right at the end.
And then there are those who I have yet to meet…

BEEN THERE

I've seen it before. I've sat at my desk with a hot ginger tea. I've watched the steam swirl up and out of the blue mug. I've turned my head to look out of the glass: the same grey sky, the same cold breeze blowing through my open window.
With the same words written onto the page of my orange Moleskine, in exactly the same order, with the same blue ink, everything seems to stop.
I'm lost in space, unable to orientate my body.
There's nothing extraordinary about this moment. It is just a moment - a speck of living.
But I've been here before, witnessed everything in minute detail: my steady breath, quickening heartbeat and an energy spinning up my spine.
There's something unsettling about this flash of déjà vu. And at the same time, quietly reassuring, familiar.
A million possibilities come flying out of this twice-lived moment.
I can't help but wonder what I would do differently if I knew for sure what was coming around the corner? Would I change my words, my actions, my hopes?
As much as we want everything to be perfect, life is also about making mistakes. Without them, we would

never grow. We would never look at ourselves and never find our inner strength. Sometimes we live and learn, sometimes we don't.

There are mistakes that make us kick ourselves, and mistakes that cause us to cringe.

And then there are those that take us to another place entirely – a place where all of our dreams come true.

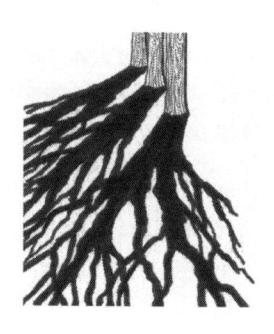

DISAPPEARING DUSK

It's already begun. No longer evening, not quite night. I'm in the space in-between where the sun gives one last push of brilliance before disappearing completely; a final flourish as the curtain comes down.
Colours grow sharper and the shadows on the grass lie elegant, long. They seem to stretch out to forever.
I glance up just as a plane full of people powers higher and higher into the sky and sweeps away from City Airport, climbing further from the ground with every second. Soon we will all just look like ants.
The light is changing. The window is closing and everything that was bathed in a hyper-real glow is starting to fade.
This is the end. And also the beginning.
I wonder about tomorrow. I wonder about the many things it holds gently in its hands for me and how with every sunset, we imperceptibly change.

The air is getting cooler now and I briefly consider going inside to grab my blue jumper when something stops me. The side of Canary Wharf is suddenly illuminated with my personal sunset. It happens most evenings and only ever lasts for a few minutes, but every single time, I'm awe-struck. Feeling my lungs fill with air, a wave of hope washes over me as I realise how much potential there is within each and every one of us.

The shadows on the grass below have now disappeared into the dusk and in a moment I will pick up my cup and head inside. The door will close and the blind will be pulled across. The lamp will go on and tea will be poured. But right now I am blinded by the reflection of the sun.

And it is beautiful.

SPECTACULAR SPECTACLES

"Can I help you find somewhere?" the voice behind us speaks in a soft Portuguese accent. We must look a little lost in this new city - this city that I'm starting to fall in love with. I turn around to see a beautiful woman with a warm smile standing there. Our guardian angel chuckles to hear that we are looking for the 'Museu dos Óculos'. She puts us back on track and waves us on our way.

Eventually, we find ourselves walking in through the door of a stunning white and blue house lifted straight out of 1900's Italy which has since been converted into an opticians. After a few words with the receptionist I am relieved to discover that the museum lies just up some wooden stairs.

We are soon greeted in Portuguese by Ivani, a middle-aged woman with reddish curly hair. She has a warm face and an infectious laugh.

And so she walks and talks. We journey through the ages past silver monocles and ivory fans, across the 60's, 70's, 80's, and up to the designer sunglasses found in Vogue magazine today.

There is something very lovely about this woman; we instantly have a connection.

After our personal tour I find out that she has been curating the free museum for over 17 years now with the love of her life. She gave up being the journalist for the Mayor of São Paulo and this was her personal collection.

We thank her for the tour as she gives us a tight hug. Suddenly she tips her head and says "coffee?"

Over steaming espressos, we talk about travel, fate, and my love of Brazilian telenovelas. It was a perfect afternoon. We laughed a lot.

Then with one last hug we say goodbye to our new friend. She wishes us happiness on our journey and I'm suddenly touched by her kindness.

Walking out into the blazing afternoon sun once more, I can't help but smile.

It's strange where life can take us sometimes. The places we go and the people we meet along the way change us forever. And that afternoon, it only took 700 pairs of glasses to see that these little random moments are what makes this big crazy world so utterly beautiful.

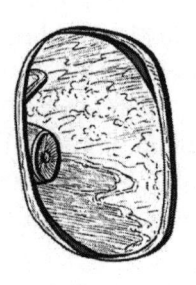

CHANGING FLIGHTS

We stop walking and I plop the bags down at my feet. The goodbye. Surrounded by travellers and trolleys, the airport continues to buzz around us. It only feels like yesterday that I was walking out of this terminal into the warm evening air of São Paulo for the first time. Everything was new and exciting. Now it feels like home. I hate goodbyes the most. And so, with my wall up and a smile on my face, I give my friend a tight hug and thank her for a wonderful three months in her crazy city. Pushing back a tear I tell her I love her, that I will be back soon, and turn to walk through security. I don't look back.
38,000ft high above the Atlantic Ocean once again, I watch the remaining rays of evening sun burn out over the wing and slowly disappear beneath the horizon. It's that moment when I know there is only a few seconds of light left before another day comes to a close. The other passengers are settled in for the night. Some are already covered in blankets, others shuffling pages of a magazine. But I am looking out

across the sky. Constellations begin to come into focus through my frozen window, and once again I am lost in the night. High above the earth, invisible to everyone below.

Despite stories from loved ones, the city embraced me and kept me safe in her arms the entire time. And as the opening credits of a movie begin to fade in and out on the little screen in front of me, I can't help but wonder how this trip has changed me. Every journey in life takes us to a different place. Sometimes the changes are obvious, and others, so subtle that we can't quite put our finger on what is different within us. But whether we like it or not, change is inevitable. And once we embrace that, we become free of the past to live in the moment; free to sit back, relax, and enjoy the flight.

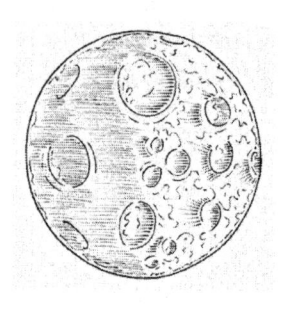

ALIGNMENT

I was 2 when it last happened.

I might have been cuddling with my mum on the sofa or playing make-believe in my wigwam; laughing, crying or smearing chocolate around my little mouth. I was completely unaware of the celestial show happening just up in the sky. The lifelong scar that now sits on my body was barely a few months old.

38 years later, I am watching the moon rise slowly in the sky. It's lifting away from the trees and up into the night. It bathes everything it touches in a silvery light. The hedges at the end of the field begin to disappear, and trees transform into gnarly silhouettes.

As we dance and spin through the blackness of space, we find ourselves, once again, next to a Christmas full moon. I sit on the bed looking out of the window with soft beams falling gently on my face…and I breathe.

There are times in our life when everything is in tune

and perfectly aligned - all is well in our wonderful world. Then there are moments when the rug gets pulled from under our feet and we struggle to simply get through the day - we are left disorientated, unable to see beyond the trees.
But it's all about letting go and believing; having faith that everything will work out in the end. And just like this coming full moon on a Christmas day, some things will only ever happen when the time is right.

FIRST

Walking out into early morning, the sleepy blue sky begins to wake. It is literally freezing. At some point during the night, whilst I was fast asleep, the first few flakes of snow fell silently to earth. The light bouncing off the crisp whiteness bathes me in its glistening glow. And then I hear it, I feel it - the sensation that suddenly floods my body with utter joy: snow crunching and compacting under my feet. Being one of my secret pleasures in life, I begin to smile as I take a deep in-breath of air and watch as a cloud of warmth leaves my body and vanishes just as quickly. With the realisation that this is the first snow of the year, I begin to think about all the other firsts in my life: the first time I came to this bustling city, alone...the first time I sat on a plane and watched the ground drift away...the first time I ate gelato...the first kiss...the first time I found love and the first time I lost it.

Life is littered with firsts and, as constantly changing as the world is, that will never change. There are endless opportunities for new beginnings everywhere, and as I continue on my journey, I suddenly feel excited for all the firsts that are yet to come.

SILENT WHITE

With a mighty push, the snow beneath you crunches and you're off. Quickly gaining momentum, the icy winter air hits your face and almost takes your breath away. Trees start to blur all around as adrenaline rushes through every part of your body. You are completely liberated - just you and your sledge gliding gracefully downwards.
Feeling the sledge begin to lose speed, I would always lurch to the side and come rolling off with dramatic flair to highlight the end of the journey. With snow still clumped heavily in my hat, I would turn and make my way back to the top once again, one step at a time. This was always the longest part of the adventure. Faithfully dragging the sledge behind me, I couldn't wait to push off at the top to fly like a bird.
Years later, I feel that same shift in the air and know that the season is transforming once again. Snow is getting ready to fall bringing with it a change of

scenery.

A part of me smiles at the chaos that is caused by the silent arrival of snow. Cars begin to slow down, trains stop running and the city gets just that little bit quieter.

As children, waking up to a blanket of snow was the most exciting thing in the world, ever! Every street corner became a playground and each untouched layer of crisp, white snow was an open invitation to run through it with wild abandon.

Snow brings with it a subtle reminder to look for every shining piece of fun in life and enjoy each moment.

Take the time to build the snowman you haven't seen for years, and make him smile.

CLICK, FLASH

A generation gone stares back at me through a sepia-toned window. As soon as I open the dusty album, images and associations splash silently over me. Relatives I once knew and loved smile joyfully through the lens, straight into my heart. Some proudly wearing medal-embellished uniforms, others sporting the latest beehive hairdos equally as proud.
I look on as page after page reveals another connection to my past, another piece of the puzzle. And then, just as I am beginning to get lost on this little trip, a wave of melancholy gently washes over me as I am reminded of how fleeting everything is. Life seems to go by at such velocity these days, we can sometimes forget to take the moment to stop and notice all the amazing things that surround us: people we love, the random acts of kindness, lessons learnt. We click and capture those precious memories that act as a witness to our own personal journey, and despite being utterly powerless to alter our past, there is a freedom in the knowledge that we still have today - a chance to grow, to change, to fly.

And as I optimistically turn the final page of this dusty collection, I can't help but wonder about all the albums that are yet to come. Pages of moments that will last an eternity.

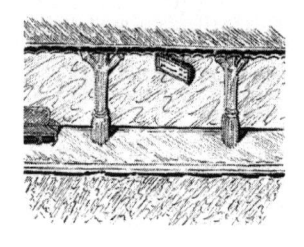

HOMEWARD BOUND

As the train speeds through the tunnel, music floats into my ears. Scenes from earlier splash into my mind and begin to overlap: my friend's sweet little boy roaring like a monster; her lovely twin daughters randomly discussing Hula Hoops. We reminisced about days gone by and laughed at the rain that began to fall lightly over our picnic.

Then I suddenly remember the old man playing a piano in the main concourse of St Pancras station just moments before we said goodbye. We stood there transfixed, him lost in his music, us lost in him.

My reverie speeds up time and before I know it, I am standing on the wet evening platform once again, close to home. I watch the train disappear into the distance and suddenly realise that there is no one else around. I feel the light drizzle on my face and stand looking up into a night sky. Right at this moment, my friend and her family are gliding out of the city, whilst the piano man is dozing peacefully as his train sways onwards.

And as I walk down the length of the platform towards the stairs, a thought occurs to me: even if I had wanted to, with all the will in the world, I couldn't have orchestrated this exact moment: the piano man, the picnic in the rain, the sound of wind picking up; the piece of rubbish blowing lightly down the platform and the plane ascending overhead. A convergence of little moments that simply happen. And all it takes is a second - a second to stop, a moment to realise that we have so much more to be grateful for than we will ever know.
And everything is beautiful.

ABOUT THE AUTHOR

Jeff is a journalist and blogger living in London. Trained as an actor, he's worked for almost 2 decades in theatre, film and TV. His weekly blog 'malleablereality.com' takes the reader on a journey through the everyday/ordinary to discover the life lessons hidden in every moment.

ABOUT THE ILLUSTRATOR

Sean Stannard studied Fine Art at Central Saint Martins and is now a freelance illustrator/comic book artist. He takes commissions from around the world. If you are interested in contacting him, email:
seanstannard99@aol.com

If you would like to message Jeff about this book or the blog, email:
jeffchandler00@aol.com

Love and Light!

Printed in Great Britain
by Amazon.co.uk, Ltd.,
Marston Gate.